ELIZABETH ONSTENK.

feature
pecially
ents

NUMBER ONE HITS

TAKE THE LEAD

violin

International MUSIC Publications

International Music Publications Limited
Griffin House 161 Hammersmith Road London W6 8BS England

Series Editor: Sadie Cook

Editorial, production and recording: Artemis Music Limited
Design and production: Space DPS Limited

Published 2000

International MUSIC Publications

© International Music Publications Limited
Griffin House 161 Hammersmith Road London W6 8BS England

International Music Publications Limited

England: Griffin House
161 Hammersmith Road
London W6 8BS

Germany: Marstallstr. 8
D-80539 München

Denmark: Danmusik
Vognmagergade 7
DK1120 Copenhagen K

Italy: Nuova Carisch Srl
Via Campania 12
20098 San Giuliano Milanese
Milano

Spain: Nueva Carisch España
Magallanes 25
28015 Madrid

France: Carisch Musicom
25 Rue d'Hauteville
75010 Paris

WARNER BROS. PUBLICATIONS U.S. INC.

USA: 15800 N.W. 48th Avenue
Miami, Florida 33014

Australia: 3 Talavera Road
North Ryde
New South Wales 2113

Scandinavia: P.O. Box 533
Vendevägen 85 B
S-182 15 Danderyd
Sweden

violin

TAKE THE LEAD

In the Book...

On the CD...

6

Demonstration

Backing

Believe

Words and Music by
Brian Higgins, Stuart McLennan, Paul Barry,
Stephen Torch, Matt Gray and Tim Powell

When You Say Nothing At All

Words and Music by
Paul Overstreet and Don Schlitz

Demonstration

Backing

Careless Whisper

Words and Music by
George Michael and Andrew Ridgeley

Demonstration   Backing

Dancing Queen

Words and Music by Benny Andersson,
Stig Anderson and Björn Ulvaeus

Demonstration

Backing

Flying Without Wings

Words and Music by
Steve Mac and Wayne Hector

I Will Always Love You

Words and Music by
Dolly Parton

Livin' La Vida Loca

Words and Music by
Robi Rosa and Desmond Child

You Needed Me

Demonstration

Backing

Words and Music by
Randy Goodrum

You can be the featured soloist with
TAKE THE LEAD

Now you can be the feature clarinet soloist on eight specially recorded arrangements

TAKE THE LEAD

clarinet

FEATURES
- Full backings to play along with
- Full demonstration tracks to help you learn the songs
- Carefully selected and edited arrangements
- Chord symbols in concert pitch

MOVIE HITS

llect these titles, each with demonstration and full backing tracks on CD.

90s Hits	Movie Hits	TV Themes	Christmas Songs
That I Breathe (Simply Red)	**Because You Loved Me** (Up Close And Personal)	**Coronation Street**	The Christmas Song
(Robbie Williams)	**Blue Monday** (The Wedding Singer)	**I'll Be There For You** (theme from *Friends*)	(Chestnuts Roasting On An Open Fir
I Live (LeAnn Rimes)	**(Everything I Do)**	**Match Of The Day**	Frosty The Snowman
Want To Miss A Thing (Aerosmith)	**I Do It For You** (Robin Hood: Prince Of Thieves)	**(Meet) The Flintstones**	Have Yourself A Merry Little Christm
here For You (The Rembrandts)	**I Don't Want To Miss A Thing** (Armageddon)	**Men Behaving Badly**	Little Donkey
t Will Go On (Celine Dion)	**I Will Always Love You** (The Bodyguard)	**Peak Practice**	Rudolph The Red-Nosed Reindeer
ng About The Way	**Star Wars (Main Title)** (Star Wars)	**The Simpsons**	Santa Claus Is Comin' To Town
k Tonight (Elton John)	**The Wind Beneath My Wings** (Beaches)	**The X-Files**	Sleigh Ride
(Madonna)	**You Can Leave Your Hat On** (The Full Monty)		Winter Wonderland
Order ref: 6725A – Flute	Order ref: 6908A – Flute	Order ref: 7003A – Flute	Order ref: 7022A – Flute
Order ref: 6726A – Clarinet	Order ref: 6909A – Clarinet	Order ref: 7004A – Clarinet	Order ref: 7023A – Clarinet
rder ref: 6727A – Alto Saxophone	Order ref: 6910A – Alto Saxophone	Order ref: 7005A – Alto Saxophone	Order ref: 7024A – Alto Saxophone
Order ref: 6728A – Violin	Order ref: 6911A –Tenor Saxophone	Order ref: 7006A – Violin	Order ref: 7025A – Violin
	Order ref: 6912A – Violin		Order ref: 7026A – Piano
			Order ref: 7027A – Drums

Blues Brothers	Latin	Jazz	Swing
ught The Katy And Left Me A Mule To Ride	Bailamos	Birdland	Chattanooga Choo Choo
Gimme Some Lovin'	Cherry Pink And Apple Blossom White	Desafinado	Choo Choo Ch'Boogie
Shake A Tail Feather	Guantanamera	Don't Get Around Much Anymore	I've Got A Gal In Kalamazoo
ody Needs Somebody To Love	La Bamba	Fascinating Rhythm	In The Mood
The Old Landmark	La Isla Bonita	Misty	It Don't Mean A Thing (If It Ain't Got That Swing)
Think	Livin' La Vida Loca	My Funny Valentine	Jersey Bounce
Minnie The Moocher	Oye Mi Canto (Hear My Voice)	One O'Clock Jump	Pennsylvania 6-5000
Sweet Home Chicago	Soul Limbo	Summertime	A String Of Pearls
Order ref: 7079A - Flute	Order ref: 7259A - Flute	Order ref: 7124A - Flute	Order ref: 7235A - Flute
Order ref: 7080A - Clarinet	Order ref: 7260A - Clarinet	Order ref: 7173A - Clarinet	Order ref: 7236A - Clarinet
rder ref: 7081A - Alto Saxophone	Order ref: 7261A - Alto Saxophone	Order ref: 7174A - Alto Saxophone	Order ref: 7237A - Alto Saxophone
der ref: 7082A - Tenor Saxophone	Order ref: 7364A - Piano	Order ref: 7175A - Tenor Saxophone	Order ref: 7238A - Tenor Saxophone
Order ref: 7083A - Trumpet	Order ref: 7262A - Trumpet	Order ref: 7179A - Drums	Order ref: 7239A - Trumpet
Order ref: 7084A - Violin	Order ref: 7263A - Violin	Order ref: 7178A - Piano	Order ref: 7240A - Violin
		Order ref: 7176A - Trumpet	
		Order ref: 7177A - Violin	